2023

LIFE
LIFE ULTIMATE PLANNER
COMPANION

2023

LIFE ULTIMATE PLANNER COMPANION
GOALS AND PRIORITY PLANNER

Top Tips and Tricks for Time Management and
Getting the Most from Your Life Ultimate Planner

Copyright © 2023 Cheryl Jackson.

ISBN: 978-1-960130-08-2

All rights reserved. No part of this book may be reproduced or transmitted in any form or by any means, electronic or mechanical, including photocopying, recording, or by any information storage and retrieval system, without permission in writing from the copyright owner. For information on distribution rights, royalties, derivative works, or licensing opportunities on behalf of this content or work, please contact the publisher at the address below.

Printed in the United States of America.

www.LiveLifeFullyCoaching.com

TABLE OF CONTENTS

Introduction 1

Calendar Basics for Success 3

How to Use the Life Ultimate Planner Features 7

Priority and Goal Setting 21

Set Your Goals and Priorities 27

2023 CALENDAR

JANUARY

M	T	W	T	F	S	S
						1
2	3	4	5	6	7	8
9	10	11	12	13	14	15
16	17	18	19	20	21	22
23	24	25	26	27	28	29
30	31					

FEBRUARY

M	T	W	T	F	S	S
		1	2	3	4	5
6	7	8	9	10	11	12
13	14	15	16	17	18	19
20	21	22	23	24	25	26
27	28					

MARCH

M	T	W	T	F	S	S
		1	2	3	4	5
6	7	8	9	10	11	12
13	14	15	16	17	18	19
20	21	22	23	24	25	26
27	28	29	30	31		

APRIL

M	T	W	T	F	S	S
					1	2
3	4	5	6	7	8	9
10	11	12	13	14	15	16
17	18	19	20	21	22	23
24	25	26	27	28	29	30

MAY

M	T	W	T	F	S	S
1	2	3	4	5	6	7
8	9	10	11	12	13	14
15	16	17	18	19	20	21
22	23	24	25	26	27	28
29	30	31				

JUNE

M	T	W	T	F	S	S
			1	2	3	4
5	6	7	8	9	10	11
12	13	14	15	16	17	18
19	20	21	22	23	24	25
26	27	28	29	30		

JULY

M	T	W	T	F	S	S
					1	2
3	4	5	6	7	8	9
10	11	12	13	14	15	16
17	18	19	20	21	22	23
24	25	26	27	28	29	30
31						

AUGUST

M	T	W	T	F	S	S
	1	2	3	4	5	6
7	8	9	10	11	12	13
14	15	16	17	18	19	20
21	22	23	24	25	26	27
28	29	30	31			

SEPTEMBER

M	T	W	T	F	S	S
				1	2	3
4	5	6	7	8	9	10
11	12	13	14	15	16	17
18	19	20	21	22	23	24
25	26	27	28	29	30	

OCTOBER

M	T	W	T	F	S	S
						1
2	3	4	5	6	7	8
9	10	11	12	13	14	15
16	17	18	19	20	21	22
23	24	25	26	27	28	29
30	31					

NOVEMBER

M	T	W	T	F	S	S
		1	2	3	4	5
6	7	8	9	10	11	12
13	14	15	16	17	18	19
20	21	22	23	24	25	26
27	28	29	30			

DECEMBER

M	T	W	T	F	S	S
				1	2	3
4	5	6	7	8	9	10
11	12	13	14	15	16	17
18	19	20	21	22	23	24
25	26	27	28	29	30	31

2024 CALENDAR

JANUARY
M	T	W	T	F	S	S
1	2	3	4	5	6	7
8	9	10	11	12	13	14
15	16	17	18	19	20	21
22	23	24	25	26	27	28
29	30	31				

FEBRUARY
M	T	W	T	F	S	S
			1	2	3	4
5	6	7	8	9	10	11
12	13	14	15	16	17	18
19	20	21	22	23	24	25
26	27	28	29			

MARCH
M	T	W	T	F	S	S
				1	2	3
4	5	6	7	8	9	10
11	12	13	14	15	16	17
18	19	20	21	22	23	24
25	26	27	28	29	30	31

APRIL
M	T	W	T	F	S	S
1	2	3	4	5	6	7
8	9	10	11	12	13	14
15	16	17	18	19	20	21
22	23	24	25	26	27	28
29	30					

MAY
M	T	W	T	F	S	S
		1	2	3	4	5
6	7	8	9	10	11	12
13	14	15	16	17	18	19
20	21	22	23	24	25	26
27	28	29	30	31		

JUNE
M	T	W	T	F	S	S
					1	2
3	4	5	6	7	8	9
10	11	12	13	14	15	16
17	18	19	20	21	22	23
24	25	26	27	28	29	30

JULY
M	T	W	T	F	S	S
1	2	3	4	5	6	7
8	9	10	11	12	13	14
15	16	17	18	19	20	21
22	23	24	25	26	27	28
29	30	31				

AUGUST
M	T	W	T	F	S	S
			1	2	3	4
5	6	7	8	9	10	11
12	13	14	15	16	17	18
19	20	21	22	23	24	25
26	27	28	29	30	31	

SEPTEMBER
M	T	W	T	F	S	S
						1
2	3	4	5	6	7	8
9	10	11	12	13	14	15
16	17	18	19	20	21	22
23	24	25	26	27	28	29
30						

OCTOBER
M	T	W	T	F	S	S
	1	2	3	4	5	6
7	8	9	10	11	12	13
14	15	16	17	18	19	20
21	22	23	24	25	26	27
28	29	30	31			

NOVEMBER
M	T	W	T	F	S	S
				1	2	3
4	5	6	7	8	9	10
11	12	13	14	15	16	17
18	19	20	21	22	23	24
25	26	27	28	29	30	

DECEMBER
M	T	W	T	F	S	S
						1
2	3	4	5	6	7	8
9	10	11	12	13	14	15
16	17	18	19	20	21	22
23	24	25	26	27	28	29
30	31					

INTRODUCTION

This stand alone companion to the Life Ultimate Planner serves two purposes. First, it illustrates how to use all the features of the Life Ultimate Planner.

Second, it includes a series of worksheets for planning goals around your priorities. There are also note sheets included to record important thoughts and ideas.

The practice of prioritizing and goal setting can be done at anytime. However, you may find it to be a significant yearly practice for December, so that your new year begins with intention. Setting goals around what is most important to you is far more enduring and persistent than New Year's Resolutions.

It is a fact that when you set a goal, you are more likely to meet or exceed your goal when you write it down. And, your success exponentially increases when your goals are set around life priorities.

LIFE ULTIMATE PLANNER COMPANION

This guide walks you through a proven process of prioritizing your goals. Then, the Life Ultimate Planner gives you the space to choose your daily actions with intention so you can accomplish your goals.

You begin with Calendar Basics for Success. Then, you will learn how to take advantage of the Life Ultimate Planner features for optimum success. Finally, the Priority and Goals worksheets will be clarified with suggestions for how to make the most of them in combination with your Life Ultimate Planner.

CALENDAR BASICS FOR SUCCESS

The Life Ultimate Planner was created after years of trial and error. I spent hours every year looking for a new planner with just the right format. When I couldn't find what I was looking for, I would give up and modify the planner I purchased to suit my needs. As a life and business coach for the past 15 years, I included all of the most powerful tools I have learned from coaching my clients on Time Management.

The number one thing I learned was that no one planner works for everyone. That's why the Life Ultimate Planner was designed to give you options. There will be parts of this planner that work for you and parts that will not. The best planner is the one you actually use, so take what you like and disregard the rest.

Here are three rules for scheduling and planning that will help you be successful at never missing an appointment and accomplishing more in less time:

TIP #1.

<u>Only use one calendar for scheduling appointments.</u> I use a digital calendar on my phone to schedule appointments exclusively. I use the Life Ultimate Planner only for writing today's schedule so I know how to plan my day for best results. You may choose to use only this planner for scheduling appointments. Either way, do all your scheduling in one place. That includes combining personal and business appointments. Wall calendars don't work for scheduling because of the next tip.

TIP #2

<u>Keep your scheduling calendar and planner with you at all times.</u> Think of it like your brain and a place to record commitments as soon as you make them. That is why I use my phone for scheduling. It is always with me. This Tip applies to the Life Ultimate Planner whether you use it for scheduling or time management or both.

That is the reason for including only three months of daily pages at a time. If something is scheduled beyond the three months, write it in the monthly calendar and transfer it to the appropriate quarterly planner.

TIP #3

<u>Look at your scheduling calendar and planner at least twice a day; morning and evening.</u> This may seem overly simple, but I'm

CALENDAR BASICS FOR SUCCESS

amazed how many people don't do this. I recommend spending five minutes every morning looking at your day. This is your time to make decisions and adjustments. Looking at your calendar five minutes before going to sleep reminds you what is coming up tomorrow. This will help you sleep better and set your alarm to awaken at the correct time so you are not rushed.

Twice a day is the minimum. The more you use both your calendar and planner, the more efficient and effective you will become. The Life Ultimate Planner includes a Monthly Calendar for all twelve months for planning ahead. You can find the nine subsequent months at the back of the planner. A Weekly Calendar is included for planning the focus and big happenings for the current week. Daily Sheets are for scheduling appointments and blocking time for achieving the tasks that accomplish your Weekly Focus.

HOW TO USE THE LIFE ULTIMATE PLANNER FEATURES

The following are suggestions. If you are new to time management and using a planner, I suggest you start slowly by choosing the three or four features that most appeal to you. Create calendaring and planning habits for those features. Then add a new feature as you feel ready. You are forming new habits and it takes at least 30-90 days to make a new habit become routine. You can use the Habit Tracker on the daily pages to intentionally create new time management habits.

SCHEDULING AND TASK MANAGEMENT TIPS

Schedule one 30 minute weekly planning time. Pick one day a week that you consider to be the day before your week begins. Choose a time of day that works best for you and schedule it as a repeat appointment on your calendar. At the beginning of each month, schedule an additional 30 minutes to wrap up your last month and plan your next month.

Next, schedule 5-10 minutes first thing every morning to prepare for your day ahead. Schedule another 5-10 minutes every night to prepare for tomorrow.

There will be more guidance on specific things to do during your planning times as we dig a little deeper into the individual Life Ultimate Planner pages.

There are four quarterly Life Ultimate Planner books each year. They incorporate three months each. Q1 (Winter) is January, February, March; Q2 (Spring) is April, May, June; Q3 (Summer) is July, August, September; Q4 (Fall) is October, November, December. They are available individually, or four at a time, beginning with the current quarter (whatever time of the year that is). This serves two purposes. They are easier to carry and you don't have to buy January to December only. If it is June, you can begin with Q3 and still purchase a full year.

Each Quarterly Life Ultimate Planner book includes these elements:

HOW TO USE THE LIFE ULTIMATE PLANNER FEATURES

- Current Annual Calendar
- Table of Contents
- Three Monthly Segments
- Next Year Annual Calendar
- Subsequent Nine Monthly Calendars
- Books to Read
- Wish List
- Lined Note Sheets (10)
- Blank Note Sheets (10)
- Index Sheets (4)
- All Pages are Numbered

Each Monthly Segment within the Life Ultimate Planner consists of these elements:

- Monthly Calendar with Goals & Notes
- Monthly Master Success Actions Worksheet
- Weekly Planner Worksheet
- Meal Planner or Food Diary Sheet with Shopping List
- Daily Actions Sheets (7)
- Monthly Income Tracker
- Monthly Expense Tracker
- Monthly Savings Tracker
- Monthly Progress Wrap-up Sheet

LIFE ULTIMATE PLANNER COMPANION

USING THE ELEMENTS OF THE MONTHLY SEGMENTS:

Monthly Calendar with Goals & Notes

Use for month at a glance and to write in big events to remember. This is not for scheduling daily appointments.

The Goals box is for noting important milestones for your long term quarterly, semi-annual, and annual goals.

The Notes box is for important reminders for the month.

HOW TO USE THE LIFE ULTIMATE PLANNER FEATURES

Monthly Master Success Actions Worksheet

MASTER SUCCESS ACTIONS
JANUARY 2023

List 4 life areas and your goals to focus on this month:

1.
2.
3.
4.

Use this master task list for the big action steps you will commit to do this month. They will accomplish the goals you set to improve your life in the 4 areas of focus. Your daily tasks will be the small steps to accomplish these bigger steps.

DONE   SUCCESS ACTIONS

This is a worksheet for your 30 minute, once a month planning time.

Choose the priorities you want to focus on this month and choose no more than four goals to support that focus. Then, list the success actions you will include in your weekly and daily sheets. (See below for more on those sheets.) As you complete them, put the date or a check mark in the "Done" column.

Two important things to remember when creating goals:

#1 Remember: Progress, not Perfection. Progress leads to success while perfection undermines progress.

#2 Celebrate your successes. Your celebrations can be big or small. Just remember to acknowledge your hard work. It can be as simple as sharing what you accomplished with a coach or friend and doing a high five. Virtual high fives work, too.

Weekly Planner Worksheet

Use this worksheet for your 30 minute weekly planning.

You can use the daily spaces to designate blocks of time available for tasks that accomplish the goals from your Monthly Master Success Actions sheet. Or you might use it to note big things for the week you need to consider when planning appointments and tasks.

HOW TO USE THE LIFE ULTIMATE PLANNER FEATURES

Use the Priorities and Goals list for the tasks that accomplish your goals from the Monthly Master Success Actions sheet.

The Success Focus Box is for whatever motivates you. Whether that's a quote or reward or prayer, make it personal to you.

The Notes box is a place to write notes to yourself. These can include reminders, ideas, your planning times, whatever! Draw a picture or doodle. It's your space, so enjoy it.

Weekly Meal Planner or Food Diary

JANUARY 2 – 8, 2023

	BREAKFAST	LUNCH	DINNER	SNACKS
M				
T				
W				
T				
F				
S				
S				

SHOPPING LIST:

This worksheet can be used for your 30 minute, once a week meal planning or a place to keep track of what you eat each day.

LIFE ULTIMATE PLANNER COMPANION

Be creative. You can add items to your Grocery List as you use them up. Jot down new recipes you want to try and the ingredients you need to make them. Loosely planning your meals for the week, including eating out and having guests, can be very helpful.

This section helps you focus on healthy eating habits. Planning meals and shopping for groceries with intention can bring powerful health benefits.

Weekly, Monthly and Quarterly Notes Sheet

The Life Ultimate Planner includes a lot of places for note taking. Having a place for notes helps you keep everything in one place. No more lost sticky notes! And when everything is in your

HOW TO USE THE LIFE ULTIMATE PLANNER FEATURES

Life Ultimate Planner, you will keep it with you and use it more consistently.

There is an Index at the end of each quarterly planner. This is a great place to write the page, date, and topic for future reference. When you keep your planners, they become a reference library of important information and goal tracking over the years.

If you are thinking, "This is just too much structure and work," give it a try for three months. You might discover that the effort is worth the rewards you receive.

Daily Planning Sheet

This sheet is the heart of the Life Ultimate Planner. Consider using a magnetic page marker so you can quickly turn to it. Feel free to use as much or little as you need. There will be days when you use it extensively all day, then days when you don't use it at all. That's okay. The Life Ultimate Planner is supposed to be a tool. Use it to make your life better than it is without it. But don't let it become a task master to you.

If you love lists, this sheet will likely be your favorite element. Your daily Success Actions will serve you best if they include some of the tasks from the monthly Master Success Actions Worksheet.

If you love a paper calendar, use the Schedule section to schedule appointments. If you use a digital calendar to schedule, you may want to write in your schedule each morning and block out time for tasks.

The habit tracker is for keeping a new habit in the front of your mind daily. Focus on only one new habit every month or two. The #2 and #3 lines are for tracking new habits for 90 days.

TIP: New habits take 30-90 days to become a natural behavior. I recommend working on no more than one new habit a month. There are three lines with a bubble for checking your new habits daily. Think of the first line as the new habit, then the second line for the second month of a new habit and the third line as the third month of the new habit. If you want to add a new habit each month, you will be using all three lines by the third month. If you create 4-12 new habits a year that generate success… that will be amazing! Small incremental changes of habit will become long term benefits in your life.

HOW TO USE THE LIFE ULTIMATE PLANNER FEATURES

Income Tracker, Expense Tracker, and Saving Tracker Tips

JANUARY 2023 INCOME TRACKER

DATE	INCOME	CATEGORY	AMOUNT
TOTAL			

JANUARY 2023 EXPENSE TRACKER

DATE	EXPENSE	CATEGORY	AMOUNT
TOTAL			

JANUARY 2023 SAVINGS TRACKER

SAVING FOR: GOAL AMOUNT:

DATE	NOTES	AMOUNT	BALANCE
TOTAL			

17

LIFE ULTIMATE PLANNER COMPANION

These are included in the Life Ultimate Planner for when your priorities include finances. If you are self-employed, they can become references you can use for your taxes, as well. If you have an expense account, they are helpful for reports. If you just want to budget and keep track of how you are doing, they will help with that, too.

Monthly Progress Sheet

MONTHLY PROGRESS - JANUARY 2023

I HAVE ACHIEVED...

I AM THANKFUL...

I'D LIKE TO IMPROVE...

HOW I WILL CELEBRATE WHAT I DID WELL...

This sheet is included at the end of each month. You can also use it during your monthly 30 minute planning.

Evaluating your progress is vital to motivation and long-term successful time management. It is an opportunity to consider

HOW TO USE THE LIFE ULTIMATE PLANNER FEATURES

and record what went well and what adjustments would make next month go better.

Celebrating success may seem natural to you. But for many, it is a new concept. Acknowledging your successes is absolutely the most important thing you can do for yourself every month. A celebration can be simply sharing your success with an accountability partner, co-worker, or boss. It can also be giving yourself a literal pat on the back and acknowledging your feelings out loud. Dance to a favorite song or reward yourself with something you have been planning to do. Just attach the action to celebrating your success!

A Message from Cheryl:

Your Weekly 30 Minute Planning times, plus the additional 30 Minute Monthly Planning times are the most important two and a half hours of the entire month. Schedule your successful time management strategy and make it a priority. The biggest obstacle to using time wisely is not taking time to look at how you are doing. Your Weekly and Monthly Planning times will allow you to make any adjustments needed before something becomes an issue.

Progress toward a goal is a success and is always worthy of celebrating. A monthly habit of looking back to evaluate and adjust, as well as planning forward, is powerful to living life on your terms. Your life will become more about doing what matters most to you. It will also free up time and provide you the focus to make everyday count.

I hope you find the Life Ultimate Planner a great tool that will help you live your life without stress and regret. I have been practicing these time management skills for thirty-five years. I have seen the most progress and serenity when I made it a priority to use these tools consistently. I know you will, too.

I would love to hear your stories and your comments. Please reach out to me through my website. Remember to be gentle with yourself and allow time to make the Life Ultimate Planner work for you. Take what you like and what works for you and disregard what does not work for you. This Planner was designed to consider Body, Mind, and Spirit. The whole person is much stronger than the sum of its parts. Everyone is different and no one process works for everyone. The Life Ultimate Planner is designed to provide elements that work for anyone, but certainly not all elements will work for everyone.

Let us be agents of change in the world by changing and making the most of our own world first.

Cheers to living your best life!

Cheryl Jackson
Time Management Coach
LiveLifeFullyCoaching.com

PRIORITY AND GOAL SETTING

HOW TO USE THESE FEATURES TO LIVE YOUR LIFE WITH INTENTION

The following pages will help you record and access your path to living a life of purpose with intention. I suggest doing this exercise once a year, then reviewing it quarterly to evaluate and make necessary changes. You will also want to use it in your monthly planning hour to complete the Monthly Master Success Actions Worksheet.

Whatever you do daily is what will become the life of purpose you desire.

LIFE ULTIMATE PLANNER COMPANION

Balance Wheel Sheet

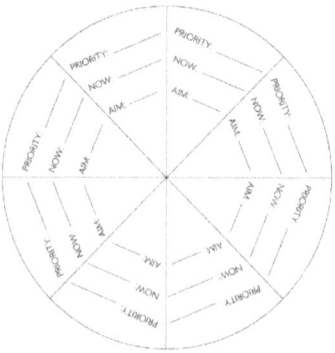

The Balance Wheel Sheet is designed to help you to identify the top priorities in your life. There are eight pieces of pie to use. You may use all eight, but it is perfectly acceptable to use fewer. More than eight can lead to lack of clarity and confusion about priorities.

Read and follow the How It Works section above the wheel for specifics on completing the Balance Wheel Sheet.

The value of this sheet is to help you direct your goals toward your priorities for life.

PRIORITY AND GOAL SETTING

Goals and Priorities Worksheets

GOALS AND PRIORITIES

HOW IT WORKS?

After analyzing the areas of life from your balance wheel, write down the necessary goals that will help improve your life. Use the numbers to rank them by priority as you aim them to be. You may do short- and long-term goals. Use the smart goals worksheet to help. Only use the categories that pertain to your priorities.

RELATIONSHIPS	1 2 3 4 5 6 7 8 9 10
FINANCIAL	1 2 3 4 5 6 7 8 9 10
CAREER	1 2 3 4 5 6 7 8 9 10
HEALTH	1 2 3 4 5 6 7 8 9 10
SPIRITUAL	1 2 3 4 5 6 7 8 9 10
PERSONAL GROWTH	1 2 3 4 5 6 7 8 9 10
REST/FUN/HOBBIES	1 2 3 4 5 6 7 8 9 10
FAMILY	1 2 3 4 5 6 7 8 9 10
PHYSICAL ENVIRONMENT	1 2 3 4 5 6 7 8 9 10
	1 2 3 4 5 6 7 8 9 10
	1 2 3 4 5 6 7 8 9 10
	1 2 3 4 5 6 7 8 9 10

These two sheets help with identifying and naming priority categories and to record your goals in those categories. The categories on these sheets are just suggestions. There are also blank spaces for writing in your own categories. The numbers are for recording the priority you aim for them to be in your life. Circle, or color that in. The blank space is for writing what goals you want to accomplish in the priority area of your life. You may use the Goal Setting Worksheets to do this.

If you are new to goal setting, I suggest one short term goal per category. Think in terms of the whole year to accomplish them. You will work on different priorities at different times during the year. The goal setting worksheet will help you with setting realistic time frames for your goals.

Also, remember that goals are not action steps. Goals are attainable things you want to accomplish that make a difference in your life. Action steps accomplish your goal. Here's an example.

Goal: Take a family vacation in August this year.

Action Steps:

- Determine (with the family) where to go for an August vacation.
- Determine and budget the cost of the vacation and time to prepare for the vacation.
- Save money for the vacation.
- Get a side hustle to help save for the vacation.
- Get buy-in from other family members to help with saving for the vacation.
- Make reservations, buy clothes, etc, etc…

Only the Goal goes on this Priorities Worksheet. Write your action steps on the Goal Setting Worksheet.

Goal Setting Worksheet

GOAL SETTING WORKSHEET

This is a worksheet provided to help you with setting smart goals for the annual goals worksheet that follows. Ensure each goal is written with these five elements. Have your "why" include your priorities from the balance wheel. Goals are achieved by action steps.

SPECIFIC (CONCISE, TO THE POINT)
MEASURABLE (SO YOU KNOW WHEN YOU HAVE ACHIEVED IT)
ATTAINABLE (STRETCHES YOU, BUT NOT SO BIG AS TO BE IMPOSSIBLE)
RELATED TO WHAT IS IMPORTANT TO YOU (PRIORITY, VISION, MISSION)
TIME LIMIT (SET A DATE ON THE CALENDAR)

SMART GOAL

WHY IS THIS IMPORTANT TO ME?

WHAT SUCCESS ACTIONS WILL ACHIEVE THIS GOAL?

HOW WILL I FEEL WHEN I ACHIEVE MY GOAL?

Use the SMART formula for writing out goals that make your priorities a reality.

You may want to write them on a separate piece of paper until you have the wording the way you want it and to check it through the SMART acronym. Then write them on your worksheet.

Your Why is related to your priorities on the balance wheel. Think of it as a "so that" statement. For the example above, "Take a family vacation in August this year - so that - our family can relax and enjoy quality time together."

The Success Actions section is the place to write your action steps to accomplish your goal.

The How Will I Feel section helps you make an emotional connection to your outcome by identifying and naming the feeling of achieving your goal.

Consider using a separate worksheet for each area of your life that is a priority for you. When you do this, it will be like aiming an arrow at a target in the direction you want your life to go. Only focus on one to three goals a month.

Goals need timeframes. Try setting a few short term one to three month goals to begin. Then stretch to six month and one year goals. Once you experience the progress that happens, you will naturally want to set longer three, five, and maybe even ten year goals. Remember, even those long term goals require shorter milestone goals to get you to the BHAGs (Big Hairy Audacious Goals).

Pick one day a week and spend 30 minutes planning your week and take part of that time to review your priorities and goals. This will keep them top of mind.

Visualize how different your life will be when you intentionally use the time you have been given to accomplish what is most important to you. Your goals and priorities will be indelibly imprinted into your mind and serve as targets you will attain.

SET YOUR GOALS AND PRIORITIES

BALANCE WHEEL

DATE: _____

HOW IT WORKS?

Think about your life as eight (or fewer) priority areas. (You may use the goals and priorities worksheet for possible priorities) Next, write a name for that priority at the top of each piece. Then evaluate the actual priority of each area on a 10-point system. Write that number next to "NOW." Then analyze and decide if that is the priority you aim for it to be. Next, write the number you "AIM" it to be.

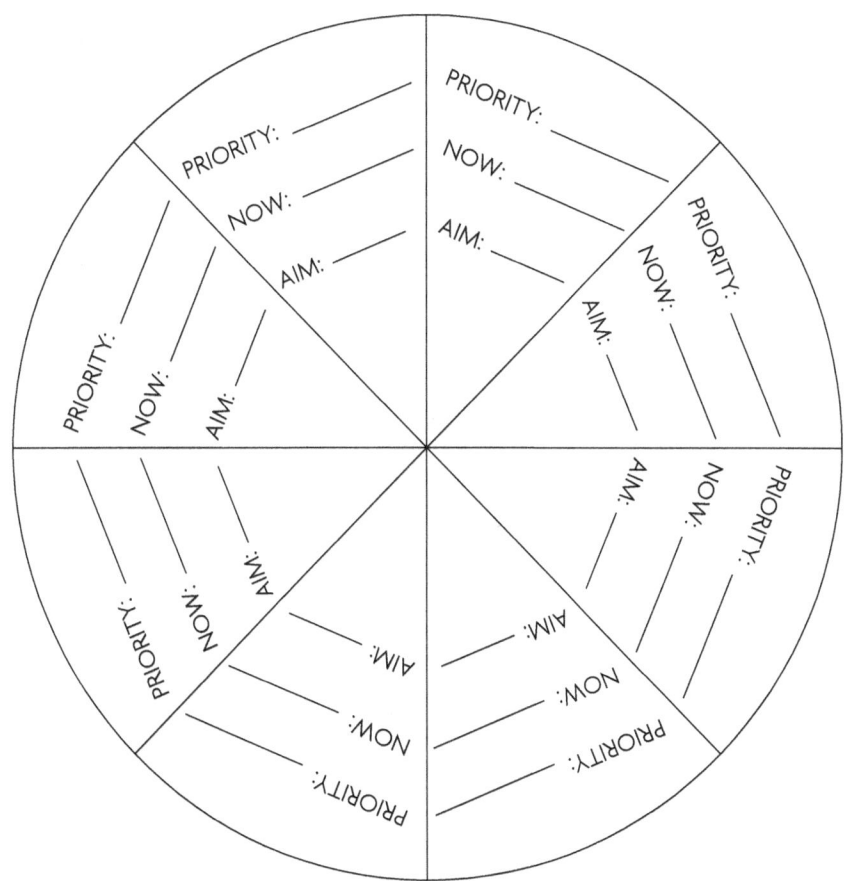

GOALS AND PRIORITIES

HOW IT WORKS?

After analyzing the areas of life from your balance wheel, write down the necessary goals that will help improve your life. Use the numbers to rank them by priority as you aim them to be. You may do short- and long-term goals. Use the smart goals worksheet to help. Only use the categories that pertain to your priorities.

RELATIONSHIPS | 1 | 2 | 3 | 4 | 5 | 6 | 7 | 8 | 9 | 10

FINANCIAL | 1 | 2 | 3 | 4 | 5 | 6 | 7 | 8 | 9 | 10

CAREER | 1 | 2 | 3 | 4 | 5 | 6 | 7 | 8 | 9 | 10

HEALTH | 1 | 2 | 3 | 4 | 5 | 6 | 7 | 8 | 9 | 10

SPIRITUAL | 1 | 2 | 3 | 4 | 5 | 6 | 7 | 8 | 9 | 10

PERSONAL GROWTH | 1 | 2 | 3 | 4 | 5 | 6 | 7 | 8 | 9 | 10

REST/FUN/HOBBIES | 1 | 2 | 3 | 4 | 5 | 6 | 7 | 8 | 9 | 10

FAMILY | 1 | 2 | 3 | 4 | 5 | 6 | 7 | 8 | 9 | 10

PHYSICAL ENVIRONMENT | 1 | 2 | 3 | 4 | 5 | 6 | 7 | 8 | 9 | 10

| 1 | 2 | 3 | 4 | 5 | 6 | 7 | 8 | 9 | 10

| 1 | 2 | 3 | 4 | 5 | 6 | 7 | 8 | 9 | 10

| 1 | 2 | 3 | 4 | 5 | 6 | 7 | 8 | 9 | 10

GOAL SETTING WORKSHEET

This is a worksheet provided to help you with setting smart goals for the annual goals worksheet that follows. Ensure each goal is written with these five elements. Have your "why" include your priorities from the balance wheel. Goals are achieved by action steps.

SPECIFIC (CONCISE, TO THE POINT)
MEASURABLE (SO YOU KNOW WHEN YOU HAVE ACHIEVED IT)
ATTAINABLE (STRETCHES YOU, BUT NOT SO BIG AS TO BE IMPOSSIBLE)
RELATED TO WHAT IS IMPORTANT TO YOU (PRIORITY, VISION, MISSION)
TIME LIMIT (SET A DATE ON THE CALENDAR)

SMART GOAL

WHY IS THIS IMPORTANT TO ME?

WHAT SUCCESS ACTIONS WILL ACHIEVE THIS GOAL?

HOW WILL I FEEL WHEN I ACHIEVE MY GOAL?

GOAL SETTING WORKSHEET

This is a worksheet provided to help you with setting smart goals for the annual goals worksheet that follows. Ensure each goal is written with these five elements. Have your "why" include your priorities from the balance wheel. Goals are achieved by action steps.

SPECIFIC (CONCISE, TO THE POINT)
MEASURABLE (SO YOU KNOW WHEN YOU HAVE ACHIEVED IT)
ATTAINABLE (STRETCHES YOU, BUT NOT SO BIG AS TO BE IMPOSSIBLE)
RELATED TO WHAT IS IMPORTANT TO YOU (PRIORITY, VISION, MISSION)
TIME LIMIT (SET A DATE ON THE CALENDAR)

SMART GOAL

WHY IS THIS IMPORTANT TO ME?

WHAT SUCCESS ACTIONS WILL ACHIEVE THIS GOAL?

HOW WILL I FEEL WHEN I ACHIEVE MY GOAL?

GOAL SETTING WORKSHEET

This is a worksheet provided to help you with setting smart goals for the annual goals worksheet that follows. Ensure each goal is written with these five elements. Have your "why" include your priorities from the balance wheel. Goals are achieved by action steps.

SPECIFIC (CONCISE, TO THE POINT)
MEASURABLE (SO YOU KNOW WHEN YOU HAVE ACHIEVED IT)
ATTAINABLE (STRETCHES YOU, BUT NOT SO BIG AS TO BE IMPOSSIBLE)
RELATED TO WHAT IS IMPORTANT TO YOU (PRIORITY, VISION, MISSION)
TIME LIMIT (SET A DATE ON THE CALENDAR)

SMART GOAL

WHY IS THIS IMPORTANT TO ME?

WHAT SUCCESS ACTIONS WILL ACHIEVE THIS GOAL?

HOW WILL I FEEL WHEN I ACHIEVE MY GOAL?

GOAL SETTING WORKSHEET

This is a worksheet provided to help you with setting smart goals for the annual goals worksheet that follows. Ensure each goal is written with these five elements. Have your "why" include your priorities from the balance wheel. Goals are achieved by action steps.

SPECIFIC (CONCISE, TO THE POINT)
MEASURABLE (SO YOU KNOW WHEN YOU HAVE ACHIEVED IT)
ATTAINABLE (STRETCHES YOU, BUT NOT SO BIG AS TO BE IMPOSSIBLE)
RELATED TO WHAT IS IMPORTANT TO YOU (PRIORITY, VISION, MISSION)
TIME LIMIT (SET A DATE ON THE CALENDAR)

SMART GOAL

WHY IS THIS IMPORTANT TO ME?

WHAT SUCCESS ACTIONS WILL ACHIEVE THIS GOAL?

HOW WILL I FEEL WHEN I ACHIEVE MY GOAL?

GOAL SETTING WORKSHEET

This is a worksheet provided to help you with setting smart goals for the annual goals worksheet that follows. Ensure each goal is written with these five elements. Have your "why" include your priorities from the balance wheel. Goals are achieved by action steps.

SPECIFIC (CONCISE, TO THE POINT)
MEASURABLE (SO YOU KNOW WHEN YOU HAVE ACHIEVED IT)
ATTAINABLE (STRETCHES YOU, BUT NOT SO BIG AS TO BE IMPOSSIBLE)
RELATED TO WHAT IS IMPORTANT TO YOU (PRIORITY, VISION, MISSION)
TIME LIMIT (SET A DATE ON THE CALENDAR)

SMART GOAL

WHY IS THIS IMPORTANT TO ME?

WHAT SUCCESS ACTIONS WILL ACHIEVE THIS GOAL?

HOW WILL I FEEL WHEN I ACHIEVE MY GOAL?

GOAL SETTING WORKSHEET

This is a worksheet provided to help you with setting smart goals for the annual goals worksheet that follows. Ensure each goal is written with these five elements. Have your "why" include your priorities from the balance wheel. Goals are achieved by action steps.

SPECIFIC (CONCISE, TO THE POINT)
MEASURABLE (SO YOU KNOW WHEN YOU HAVE ACHIEVED IT)
ATTAINABLE (STRETCHES YOU, BUT NOT SO BIG AS TO BE IMPOSSIBLE)
RELATED TO WHAT IS IMPORTANT TO YOU (PRIORITY, VISION, MISSION)
TIME LIMIT (SET A DATE ON THE CALENDAR)

SMART GOAL

WHY IS THIS IMPORTANT TO ME?

WHAT SUCCESS ACTIONS WILL ACHIEVE THIS GOAL?

HOW WILL I FEEL WHEN I ACHIEVE MY GOAL?

GOAL SETTING WORKSHEET

This is a worksheet provided to help you with setting smart goals for the annual goals worksheet that follows. Ensure each goal is written with these five elements. Have your "why" include your priorities from the balance wheel. Goals are achieved by action steps.

SPECIFIC (CONCISE, TO THE POINT)
MEASURABLE (SO YOU KNOW WHEN YOU HAVE ACHIEVED IT)
ATTAINABLE (STRETCHES YOU, BUT NOT SO BIG AS TO BE IMPOSSIBLE)
RELATED TO WHAT IS IMPORTANT TO YOU (PRIORITY, VISION, MISSION)
TIME LIMIT (SET A DATE ON THE CALENDAR)

SMART GOAL

WHY IS THIS IMPORTANT TO ME?

WHAT SUCCESS ACTIONS WILL ACHIEVE THIS GOAL?

HOW WILL I FEEL WHEN I ACHIEVE MY GOAL?

GOAL SETTING WORKSHEET

This is a worksheet provided to help you with setting smart goals for the annual goals worksheet that follows. Ensure each goal is written with these five elements. Have your "why" include your priorities from the balance wheel. Goals are achieved by action steps.

SPECIFIC (CONCISE, TO THE POINT)
MEASURABLE (SO YOU KNOW WHEN YOU HAVE ACHIEVED IT)
ATTAINABLE (STRETCHES YOU, BUT NOT SO BIG AS TO BE IMPOSSIBLE)
RELATED TO WHAT IS IMPORTANT TO YOU (PRIORITY, VISION, MISSION)
TIME LIMIT (SET A DATE ON THE CALENDAR)

SMART GOAL

WHY IS THIS IMPORTANT TO ME?

WHAT SUCCESS ACTIONS WILL ACHIEVE THIS GOAL?

HOW WILL I FEEL WHEN I ACHIEVE MY GOAL?

NOTES

NOTES

NOTES

NOTES

NOTES

NOTES

NOTES

NOTES

NOTES

NOTES

www.ingramcontent.com/pod-product-compliance
Lightning Source LLC
Chambersburg PA
CBHW070551090426
42735CB00013B/3155